SING & LEARN Phonics VOL. 3

Ready-to-use reproducible worksheets and exercises teaching initial blends, common word families, digraphs and dipthongs

by Jack Brudzynski

Song lyrics: Ed P. Butts
Music: Sara Jordan (SOCAN)

ISBN: 978-1-55386-245-1

Acknowledgements

Author - Jack Brudzynski
Lyricist - Ed P. Butts
Composer - Sara Jordan (SOCAN)
Illustrator - Various Contributors
Educational Consultant - Arlene Grierson
Interior Layout - Darryl Taylor, Derek Veenhof
Cover Design - Campbell Creative Services
Editors - Joan Howard, Sara Jordan

For of individuals or institutions located in the United States, permission is given to reproduce one set for your classroom purposes. In territories other than the United States, reproduction of the whole or any part of this publication is permitted only with the express written permission of the copyright holder, or under a licence from Access Copyright, The Canadian Copyright Licensing Agency or another national reprographic rights organization.

For further information contact:

Jordan Music Productions Inc.
M.P.O. Box 490
Niagara Falls, NY
U.S.A. 14302-0490

Jordan Music Productions Inc.
R.P.O. Lakeport, Box 28105
St. Catharines, ON
Canada, L2N 7P8

telephone: 1-800-567-7733
web Site: www.sara-jordan.com
e-mail: sjordan@sara-jordan.com

© 2014 Sara Jordan and Jordan Music Productions Inc.
All rights reserved.

We acknowledge the financial support of the Government of Canada through the Book Publishing Industry Development Program (BPIDP) for our publishing activities.

Canada

Table of Contents

Chapter One — Teaching the Sound of "ch"

Group Lessons
1. "ch"s Down the Chimney...7
2. Picture Popcorn..7

Song Lyrics
Chew, Chew ("ch")..8

Individual Activities
1. Color the "ch"..9
2. Finish the Sentence..10

Chapter Two — Teaching the Sound of "sh"

Group Lessons
1. Shhhhhh! Quiet!..11
2. Bag of Sounds...11

Song Lyrics
A Wish to Share ("sh")..12

Individual Activities
1. Which Sound? "sh" or "ch"?.................................13
2. Identify by Coloring...14

Chapter Three — Teaching the Sound of "th"

Group Lessons
1. Growing Tree of Words..15
2. Matching Pairs..15

Song Lyrics
My Thumb ("th")..16

Individual Activities
1. Missing Letters..17
2. Finish the Sentence..18

Chapter Four — Teaching the Sound of "wh"

Group Lessons
1. Colored Balloons...19
2. Sound People...19

Song Lyrics
Wheels and Whales ("wh")......................................20

Individual Activities
1. Wally's Wheels..21
2. Finish the Sentence..22

Chapter Five — Teaching the Sound of "oo"

Group Lessons
1. Word Wall..23
2. Crosswords..23

Song Lyrics
"oo" Can Make Two Sounds....................................24

Individual Activities
1. Missing Letters..25
2. Finish the Sentence..26

Chapter Six — Teaching the Sound of "ng"

Group Lessons
1. Word Factory ... 27
2. Families of Words ... 27

Song Lyrics
Sing! Sing! ("ng") ... 28

Individual Activities
1. Write and Match "ng" Words ... 29
2. Cut and Paste: My Old Grandfather Clock ... 30

Chapter Seven — Teaching the Sound of "igh"

Group Lessons
1. Picture Popcorn ... 31
2. Rhyming Picture Chain ... 31

Song Lyrics
Night Light ("igh") ... 32

Individual Activities
1. Mike and his Night Light ... 33
2. Missing Letters ... 34

Chapter Eight — Teaching the Sound of "oi"

Group Lessons
1. Making Noise with "oi" and ... 35
2. Building Words ... 35

Song Lyrics
Singing "oi" Words ... 36

Individual Activities
1. Finish the Sentence ... 37
2. Birthday Party ... 38

Chapter Nine — Teaching the Sound of the Long "e"

Group Lessons
1. Rhyming Picture Chain ... 39
2. Schools of Fish in the Sea ... 39

Song Lyrics
Troy and Ray ("oy" and "ay") ... 40

Individual Activities
1. Missing Letters ... 41
2. Finish the Sentence ... 42

Chapter Ten — Teaching the Sounds of "ow" and "ou"

Group Lessons
1. Hula-Hoop Phonics ... 43
2. Baskets ... 43

Song Lyrics
Round and Round ("ow" and "ou") ... 44

Individual Activities
1. Missing Letters ... 45
2. Finish the Sentence ... 46

Chapter Eleven — Teaching the Sounds of "k", Hard "c" and Soft "c"

Group Lessons
1. Racing Cars..47
2. Who Stole the Cookies from the Cookie Jar?......................47

Song Lyrics
"k", Hard "c" and Soft "c"...48

Individual Activities
1. Clem the Cat..49
2. Crossword Puzzle...50

Chapter Twelve — Teaching the Sounds of Silent "h" and Silent "k"

Group Lessons
1. Erase the Silent Letter...51
2. Knock Knock! Who's There?..51

Song Lyrics
Knock, Knock (Silent "h" and "k")....................................52

Individual Activities
1. Missing Letters..53
2. Sorting Balloons..54

Chapter Thirteen — Review

Individual Activities
1. Knock, Knock...55
2. Sound Out the Pictures..56
3. Fill in the Missing Letters..57
4. Crossword Puzzle..58
5. Sounding Out the Pictures..59
6. Juggling Jack...60

Complete List of Words 61

TIPS FOR THE TEACHER

Hints for Teachers and Parents

Welcome aboard! We're sure you'll enjoy our "Sing and Learn" Phonics series. This comprehensive, four-part series is presently used to teach school children all over the world to read and is now being used as far away as China!

Sing and Learn Phonics was developed using the Synthetic Phonics approach. Through this method of instruction, students are introduced to the 42 different sounds of letters and letter groups. They then practice reading, through the segmenting and blending of these sounds.

Comparative studies done of various phonics programs and methods prove that students learning to read using the Synthetic Phonics approach come out well ahead. To learn more about Sing and Learn Phonics and how it aligns with the Common Core Curriculum State Standards, please visit: SongsThatTeach.com/phonics.

The songs and activities in Volume Three are based on initial blends, common word families, consonants, consonant digraphs, variant vowels, dipthongs, silent consonants, and the sound of igh. You will find that each lesson starts with two group activities. These group activities are followed by song lyrics (to be used with the accompanying CD to introduce each lesson's song).
Reproducible exercises based on the song conclude each chapter.

A few ways to use the songs, activities and exercises in this learning kit:

Before singing a song with students, we suggest that you announce the particular letter sounds to be learned that day, and have students practice identifying them in various words. Segment simple words into phonemes and then substitute new alternative phonemes to make new words. Simple c-v-c (consonant-vowel-consonant) words are used wherever possible. Studying phonics through song also utilizes the "whole language approach" allowing students to recognize sight words and to read words within the context of each song.

After a song has been sung, discuss with students what other new words they can think of that employ the same phonemes. Have students guess how these words are spelled. Advanced students will delight in using the music karaoke tracks allowing them to perform for the class or to write their own lyrics.
A word list, downloadable PDFs of picture cards, a supplemental worksheets and activities can be found by visiting our website: www.SongsThatTeach.com/phonics.

Learning to read can be an incredible journey for both student and teacher!

Sara Jordan
President

Name: _____

CHAPTER 1

Teaching the Sound of "ch"

"ch"s Down the Chimney!

Materials:
- picture cards of "ch" words
- construction paper
- scissors
- masking tape
- chalk

Preparation: This activity will require picture cards of "ch" words. You can make your own from the "word list" on page 61, or print out the PDFs found at: www.SongsThatTeach.com/phonics. Cut the picture cards out and tape them onto pieces of construction paper. On the back of each piece of construction paper, write the corresponding word. Draw a chimney using chalk and attach all the pieces around it.

How it Works: Ask volunteers to come up to the board, one at a time, select a picture card and throw it down the chimney. They are to say "I'm throwing (ch word) down the chimney" and the class responds by saying "(ch word) goes down the chimney". Alternate: Flip the picture cards over so that they only show the word.

Picture Popcorn

Materials:
- picture cards
- scissors
- timer (optional)

Preparation: This activity will require picture cards. You can make your own from the "word list" on page 61, or print out the PDFs found at: www.SongsThatTeach.com/phonics.
Only cut out the pictures that have the "ch" sound in them (optional). Laminate them (optional).

How it Works: Give each student a picture card while the class sits in a circle. Give the students a moment to look at their picture and sound out their word. When everyone is ready, one student stands up, says their word and sits back down. The adjacent student does the same and so on until every student in the circle has had their turn. Then, each student passes their picture card to the left, right or across and play again. A timer can be used as an extra challenge.

Sing and Learn Phonics, vol. 3 © 2014 Sara Jordan Publishing

CHAPTER 1

Chew, Chew ("ch")

chorus 2x:

The letters "ch" make the sound /ch/:
/ch/, /ch/, /ch/, /ch/.
The letters "ch" make the sound /ch/:
/ch/, /ch/, /ch/, /ch/.

The letters "ch" make the sound /ch/:
/ch/, /ch/, /ch/, /ch/.
The letters "ch" make the sound /ch/:
/ch/, /ch/, /ch/, /ch/.

/ch/ is the first sound in: chip, chin, cheek.
/ch/ is the middle sound of: preacher, teacher.
/ch/ is the end of: munch, lunch, bunch.
/ch/ is so common. We use it so much.

/ch/ is the first sound in: chip, chin, cheek.
/ch/ is the middle sound of: preacher, teacher.
/ch/ is the end of: munch, lunch, bunch.
/ch/ is so common. We use it so much.

ch-i-p, chip, ch-ee-k, cheek,
m-un-ch, munch, l-un-ch, lunch

Chew, chew chips.
Chew, chew cheese.
Chew, chew chips
with cheese dip please.

Chew, chew, chomp, chomp
chin and cheeks.
Chew, chew chips
and chunks of cheese.

Chew, chew chewy,
cherry pie.
Can't stop chewing –
don't know why.

I like peaches,
chew them too.
Chew and chomp.
It's good for you.

chorus 2x:

The letters "ch" make the sound /ch/:
/ch/, /ch/, /ch/, /ch/.
The letters "ch" make the sound /ch/:
/ch/, /ch/, /ch/, /ch/.

The letters "ch" make the sound /ch/:
/ch/, /ch/, /ch/, /ch/.
The letters "ch" make the sound /ch/:
/ch/, /ch/, /ch/, /ch/.

Name: _____

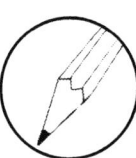

Color the Pictures with the "ch" Sound

Sound out each picture. Color the pictures that have a "ch" sound in them.

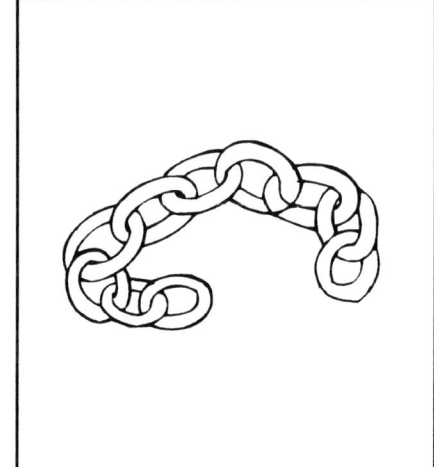

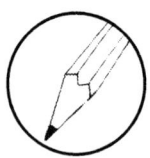

Finish the Sentence

Sound out the picture. Find the word at the bottom of the page.
Write it in the blank space. Read out the entire sentence.

Everyone sat in their _____ at the dinner table.

Jill watches television on the _____ .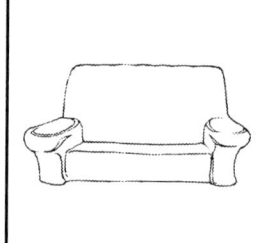

The smoke rises from out of the _____ .

Our fruit basket has four bananas, three apples and one _____ .

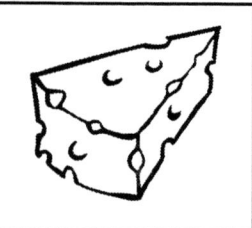

The mouse ate the _____ .

Word Bank				
couch	chair	peach	cheese	chimney

CHAPTER 2

Teaching the Sound of "sh"

Shhhhhh! Quiet!

Materials: • picture cards (optional)

Preparation: This activity will require picture cards. You can make your own from the "word list" on page 61, or print out the PDFs found at: www.SongsThatTeach.com/phonics. If copying picture cards, select all the picture cards that have the "sh" sound in them as well as a few others or simply create a list of "sh" words as well as a few others.

How it Works: Select a picture card/word. Begin by slowly sounding out the word. If the class hears the "sh" sound, they say: "Shhhhhh! Quiet! Your (sh word) is making too much noise." Repeat this activity and you may speed up the rate at which you sound out the words to make it more challenging.

Bag of Sounds

Materials:
• picture cards with "sh" and "ch" sounds
• scissors
• bag

Preparation: This activity will require picture cards. You can make your own from the "word list" on page 61, or print out the PDFs found at: www.SongsThatTeach.com/phonics. Cut them out and place them in a bag.

How it Works: Divide the class into two groups; one group for "ch" sounds, the other group for "sh" sounds. Take a picture card and sound it out. A group raises their hand when they hear their sound. Alternate: Spread the picture cards out and have the groups segregate the cards.

CHAPTER 2

A Wish to Share ("sh")

chorus:

*The letters "sh" make the sound: /sh/,
/sh/, /sh/, /sh/, /sh/.
The letters "sh" make the sound: /sh/,
/sh/, /sh/, /sh/, /sh/.*

*/sh/ is the first sound in: shall, should, share.
/sh/ is the last sound in: fresh, hush, lush.
The letters "sh" make the sound /sh/,
/sh/, /sh/, /sh/, /sh/.*

sh-all, shall, sh-are, share
w-ish, wish, h-ush, hush

These are some words
that have the sound: /sh/
/sh/, /sh/, /sh/, /sh/.

Shall I, should I
make a wish?
A wish to share,
a wish to share.

I shall try.
I won't be shy.
A wish to share
to show I care.

I wish for the sun
to shine all day.
A wish to share,
a wish to share.

But there should always
be soft shade.
A wish to share
to show I care.

I wish in the night
when the shadows fall,
a wish to share,
a wish to share,

that there shall be peace
and a hush for all.
A wish to share
to show I care.

Name: _____

Which Sound? "sh" or "ch"

Sound out each picture. In the blank space, indicate if the word has an "sh" or a "ch" sound. Color the "sh" pictures.

_____ _____ _____ _____

  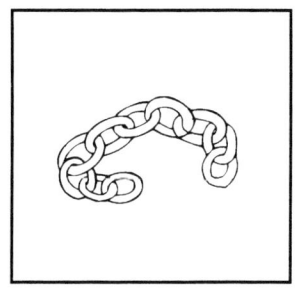 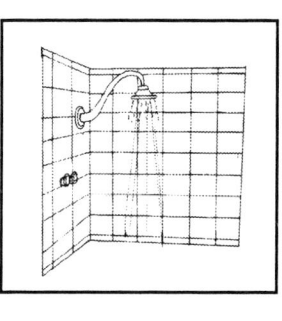

_____ _____ _____ _____

  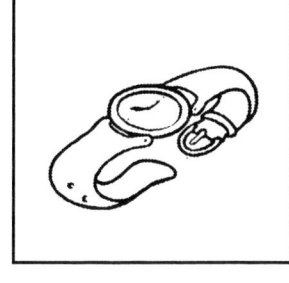 

_____ _____ _____ _____

Sing and Learn Phonics, vol. 3   © 2014 Sara Jordan Publishing   www.SongsThatTeach.com

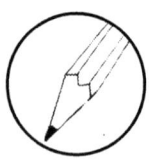

Name: _____

Identify by Coloring

Sound out each picture. Color the pictures that have a "ch" sound red.
Color the pictures that have an "sh" sound blue.

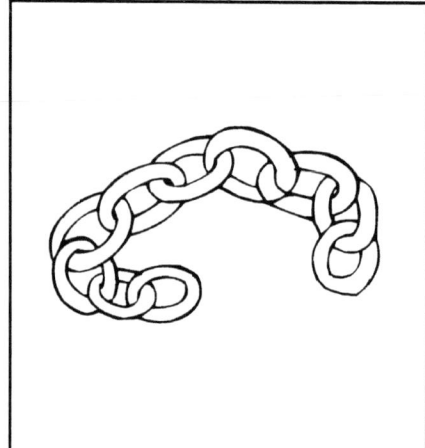

CHAPTER 3

Teaching the Sound of "th"

Growing Tree of Words

Materials: picture cards of "th" words, construction paper, scissors, masking tape, marker

Preparation: This activity will require picture cards. You can make your own from the "word list" on page 61, or print out the PDFs found at: www.SongsThatTeach.com/phonics. Cut them out and paste them on ovals cut out of green or other leaf colored construction paper. Write the corresponding word on the back of each leaf. Create a tree with branches out of construction paper or chalk.

How it Works: Hold up a leaf and ask a volunteer to read it out and attach it to the tree. Extra: Group target sounds to certain branches – this way the student must also recognize which group a leaf may belongs to.

Matching Pairs

Materials: picture cards of "sh", "ch", and "th" words, construction paper, scissors, marker

Preparation : This activity will require picture cards. You can make your own from the "word list" on page 61, or print out the PDFs found at: www.SongsThatTeach.com/phonics. Cut them out and place them in a pile. Create another pile of cards out of construction paper and write the words corresponding to the picture cards so that by the end every picture card has a word card.

How it Works: Mix both piles separately. Give each student one picture card and one word card. Have the students mingle between each other to see if they can find matching pairs, that is, a picture card and a word card for the same object. Have the student present their matching pair to you. You can also set rules, like having the students trade only word cards if one finds a match. Use a stop watch to see how long the students take to match all their cards.

CHAPTER 3

My Thumbs ("th")

chorus:

The letters "th" make the sound:
/th/, /th/, /th/.
The letters "th" make the sound:
/th/, /th/, /th/.

The letters "th" make the sound:
/th/, /th/, /th/.
The letters "th" make the sound:
/th/, /th/, /th/.

/th/ is the first sound in: that, this, thumb.
/th/ is the middle sound in: mother, brother.

th-a-t, that, th-u-mb, thumb
m-o-th-er, mother, br-o-th-er, brother

chorus:

The letters "th" make the sound:
/th/, /th/, /th/.
The letters "th" make the sound:
/th/, /th/, /th/.

The letters "th" make the sound:
/th/, /th/, /th/.
The letters "th" make the sound:
/th/, /th/, /th/.

My thumbs help me do so much.
There's so much they can do.
Throw a ball. Pull a thread.
How about you?

Sewing's easy if I wear
a thimble on my thumb.
My thumbs are nimble thanks to thimbles.
How about you?

Even though I like my toes
I can't throw a ball with those.
Thumbs help my fingers
throw humdingers.
How about you?

chorus:

The letters "th" make the sound:
/th/, /th/, /th/.
The letters "th" make the sound:
/th/, /th/, /th/.

The letters "th" make the sound:
/th/, /th/, /th/.
The letters "th" make the sound:
/th/, /th/, /th/.

Name: _____

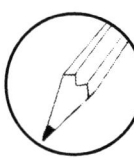

Missing Letters

Sound out each picture. Fill in the missing letters. Trace each word. Color the pictures that have a "th" sound.

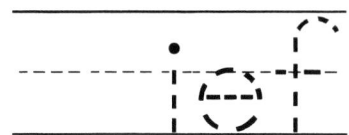

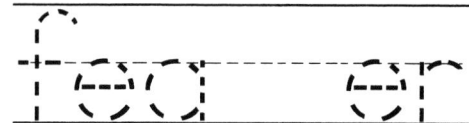

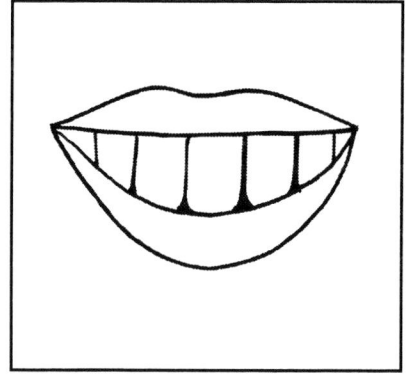

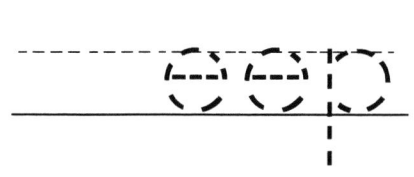
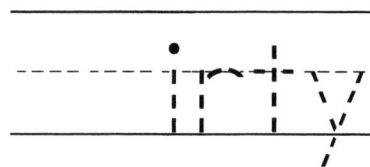

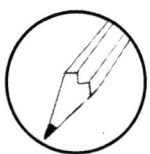

Finish the Sentence

Sound out the picture. Find the word at the bottom of the page.
Write it in the blank space. Read out the entire sentence.

 Richard has good manners.

He says "Please", _____ you and

"You're welcome."

The quiz made Anna _____ hard today.

 A _____ steals things.

When I am dirty, I take a _____ .

 The bird dropped a colorful _____ .

Word Bank				
bath	thank	feather	think	thief

CHAPTER 4

Teaching the Sound of "wh"

Colored Balloons

Materials:
- picture cards ("ch", "sh", "th" and "wh" words)
- construction paper
- scissors
- masking tape

Preparation: This activity will require picture cards. You can make your own from the "word list" on page 61, or print out the PDFs found at: www.SongsThatTeach.com/phonics. Cut out the picture cards and spread them on a table. Create four large balloons out of construction paper and tape them to the chalkboard.

How it Works: Designate a target sound to each balloon either by writing the sound on or beside the balloon. Target sounds to choose from are: "ch", "sh", "th" and "wh". Have the students sift through the picture cards and tape them to the proper balloon. Once finished, divide the class into four groups. Have volunteers from each group sound out the words in each balloon and identify the target sound in each word.

Sound People

Materials:
- construction paper
- scissors
- marker

Preparation: Create sound cards by writing sounds on pieces of construction paper.

How it Works: Distribute the sound cards to the class. Have the students mingle and blend their sounds together to try and form words. If a group of students successfully forms a word, write the word on the board. Repeat this activity as the students learn more sounds.

CHAPTER 4

Wheels and Whales ("wh")

chorus:

The letters "wh" make the sound:
/hw/, /hw/.
The letters "wh" make the sound:
/hw/, /hw/.

The letters "wh" make the sound:
/hw/, /hw/.
The letters "wh" make the sound:
/hw/, /hw/.

> The sound of the letters "wh" can also be shown as /w/ but the more common method (for most dialects) is /hw/.

spoken:

/hw/ is the first sound in wheel and whale.
/hw/ is the first sound in why and whiz.

/hw/ is the first sound in whack and whirl.
/hw/ is the first sound in whisk and when.

wh-ee-l, wheel, wh-a-le, whale
wh-a-ck, whack, wh-i-z, whiz

Why do whales
have big tails?
What are
whale tails for?

Whales whack water
with their whale tails.
That's what big
whale tails are for.

Wheels that whirl,
wheels that twirl;
where do wheels
all go?

Name: _____

Wally's Wheels

Help Wally get to the end of the road by coloring the pictures that have a "wh" sound in their names.

Finish the Sentence

Sound out the picture. Find the word that completes the sentence at the bottom of the page. Write it in the blank space. Read out the entire sentence.

The _____ is round.

This farmer grows _____ .

I hear the _____ .

The _____ is in the ocean.

 A zebra has black and _____ stripes.

Word Bank				
wheat	whale	whistle	white	wheel

CHAPTER 5

Teaching the Sounds of "oo"

Word Wall

Materials: picture cards of words containing "ŏŏ" and "ōō" sounds, construction paper, scissors, marker

Preparation: This activity will require picture cards. You can make your own from the "word list" on page 61, or print out the PDFs found at: www.SongsThatTeach.com/phonics. Cut them out and paste them on pieces of construction paper. Cut out an equal amount of blank pieces of construction paper on which you will need to write the corresponding word to each picture card creating word cards.

How it Works: Tape the word cards on the chalkboard. Students identify the word and tape their picture card beside the word card that matches it.

Alternate: Tape the picture cards on the board and have the students tape the word cards beside the picture cards.

Crosswords

Materials: picture cards, chalk

Preparation: This activity will require picture cards. You can make your own from the "word list" on page 61, or print out the PDFs found at: www.SongsThatTeach.com/phonics. Cut them out and then write in black the corresponding word on the back of them. Cut each picture card again – roughly in half and in a jagged pattern and be sure not to cut through a letter. Color the first half of word in one color and the other half another.

How it Works: Have the students sit in a semi-circle. Give each student a picture card and have them place it on the floor in front of them so that both you and the group can see it. Begin by writing a letter on the chalkboard. Ask if someone has a picture card that begins with that letter. Have the student sound out the word as you write it on the board. Draw a square around any letter of the word and ask if someone has a picture card that begins with that letter. Repeat.

CHAPTER 5

"oo" Can Make Two Sounds

chorus:

"oo" can make two sounds.
/o͝o/, /o͝o/, and /o͞o/, /o͞o/.
"oo" can make two sounds.
/o͝o/, /o͝o/, and /o͞o/, /o͞o/.

/o͝o/ in the middle of: book, look, cook
/o͞o/ in the middle of: cool, tool, fool.
"oo" can make two sounds.
/o͝o/, /o͝o/, and /o͞o/, /o͞o/.

Let's practise /o͝o/.
   I like to look
     at a very good book.
     I look at my book
     in a little book nook.

I took my book
down to the brook.
By the crook in the brook
I look at my book.

chorus:

"oo" can make two sounds.
/o͝o/, /o͝o/, and /o͞o/, /o͞o/.
"oo" can make two sounds.
/o͝o/, /o͝o/, and /o͞o/, /o͞o/.

/o͝o/ in the middle of: book, look, cook
/o͞o/ in the middle of: cool, tool, fool.
"oo" can make two sounds.
/o͝o/, /o͝o/, and /o͞o/, /o͞o/.

Let's practise /o͞o/.
   It is so cool
     to read in school,
     but the best place to read is
     by the pool.

I'm in a great mood
when I have food
and a drink that's cool
after school.

Name: _____

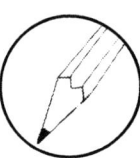

Missing Letters

Sound out each picture. Fill in the missing letters. Trace each word. Color the pictures that have an "ŏŏ" or "ōō" sound.

m__n    w__d    __ale

sch__l  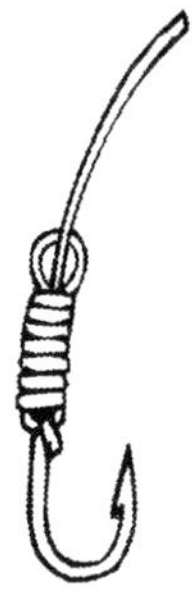   ___   __k

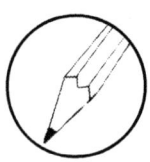

Name: _____

Finish the Sentence

Sound out each picture. Use the words at the bottom of the page to complete each of the sentences. Write them in the blank spaces. Read out the entire sentences.

 There is a full _____ tonight.

We saw many animals at the _____ .

 _____ burns in the fire.

I had fun at _____ today.

 I read a good _____ at the library.

Word Bank				
zoo	moon	wood	book	school

Teaching the Sound of "ng"

Word Factory

Materials:
- cardboard box
- construction paper
- scissors
- marker

Preparation: Place the cardboard box upside down and cut two holes in two sides that are adjacent to each other. The first hole should be large enough for you to put your hands through and the second hole should be large enough for a piece of construction paper to slide through. Cut strips of paper and write words (incorporating the "ng" sound) on them.

How it Works: Place the strips of paper inside the factory and pull one strip slowly through the second hole. Orient the box so that as you pull the strip through, the word will appear letter by letter in proper reading order (left to right). Have the students sound out each letter until the entire word is produced.

Families of Words

Materials:
- picture cards
- chalk
- masking tape

Preparation: This activity will require picture cards. You can make your own from the "word list" on page 61, or print out the PDFs found at: www.SongsThatTeach.com/phonics. Cut them out and select only the ones that belong to one of four target sounds of your choice. Draw four houses out of chalk.

How it Works: Divide the class into four groups, one for each target sound/house. Have the groups find the picture cards that belong in their house and have them tape the picture cards inside their house. When finished, each house will have a family of words; that is, many words with the same target sound. Have each group read aloud each word in their house.

CHAPTER 6

Sing! Sing! ("ng")

chorus 2x:

The letters "ng" make the sound: /ng/
/ng/, /ng/, /ng/, /ng/.
/ng/ is at the end of: strong, sung, sing.
/ng/ is at the end of: long, lung, bring.

The letters "ng" make the sound: /ng/
/ng/, /ng/, /ng/, /ng/.
/ng/ is at the end of: strong, sung, sing.
/ng/ is at the end of: long, lung, bring.

s-i-ng, sing, br-i-ng, bring
st-r-o-ng, strong, st-r-i-ng, string
l-o-ng, long, th-i-ng, thing
s-o-ng, song, r-i-ng, ring.

chorus:

The letters "ng" make the sound: /ng/
/ng/, /ng/, /ng/, /ng/.
/ng/ is at the end of: strong, sung, sing.
/ng/ is at the end of: long, lung, bring.

Sing! Sing! Sing out strong.
Sing "ng" words all day long.

Fill your lungs. Sing loud and long.
Sing! Sing! Sing this song.

chorus:

The letters "ng" make the sound: /ng/
/ng/, /ng/, /ng/, /ng/.
/ng/ is at the end of: strong, sung, sing.
/ng/ is at the end of: long, lung, bring.

Sing! Sing! Sing out strong.
The gang will sing all day long.

And when this song has been sung,
we will sing another one.

chorus:

The letters "ng" make the sound: /ng/
/ng/, /ng/, /ng/, /ng/.
/ng/ is at the end of: strong, sung, sing.
/ng/ is at the end of: long, lung, bring.

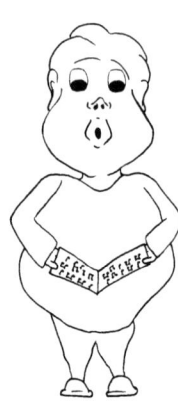

Name: _____

Write and Match "ng" Words

Sound out all the pictures. Fill in the blank spaces by writing the words supplied below. Draw a line from the word to the corresponding picture.

___ng

___ng

___ng

___ng

___ng

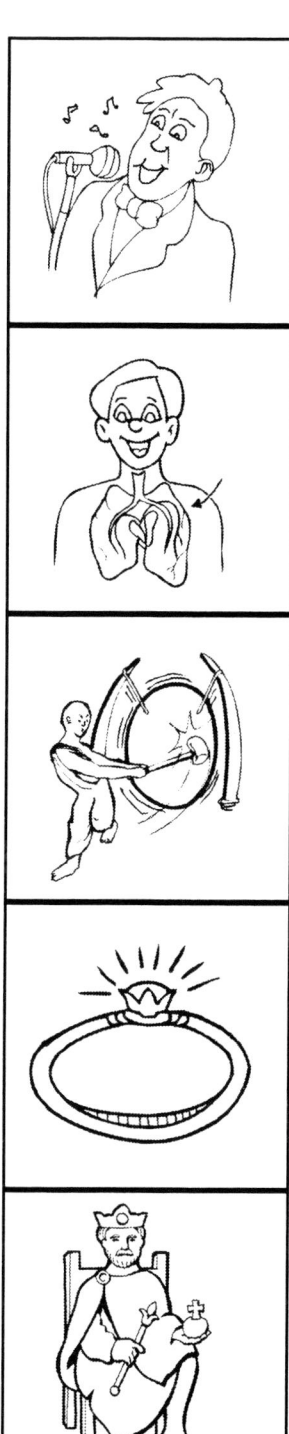

Word Bank
sing   lung   ring   gong   king

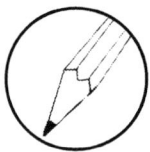

Cut and Paste: My Old Grandfather Clock

Sound out the pictures and color them.

Cut and paste the pictures that have an "ng" sound in the grandfather clock.

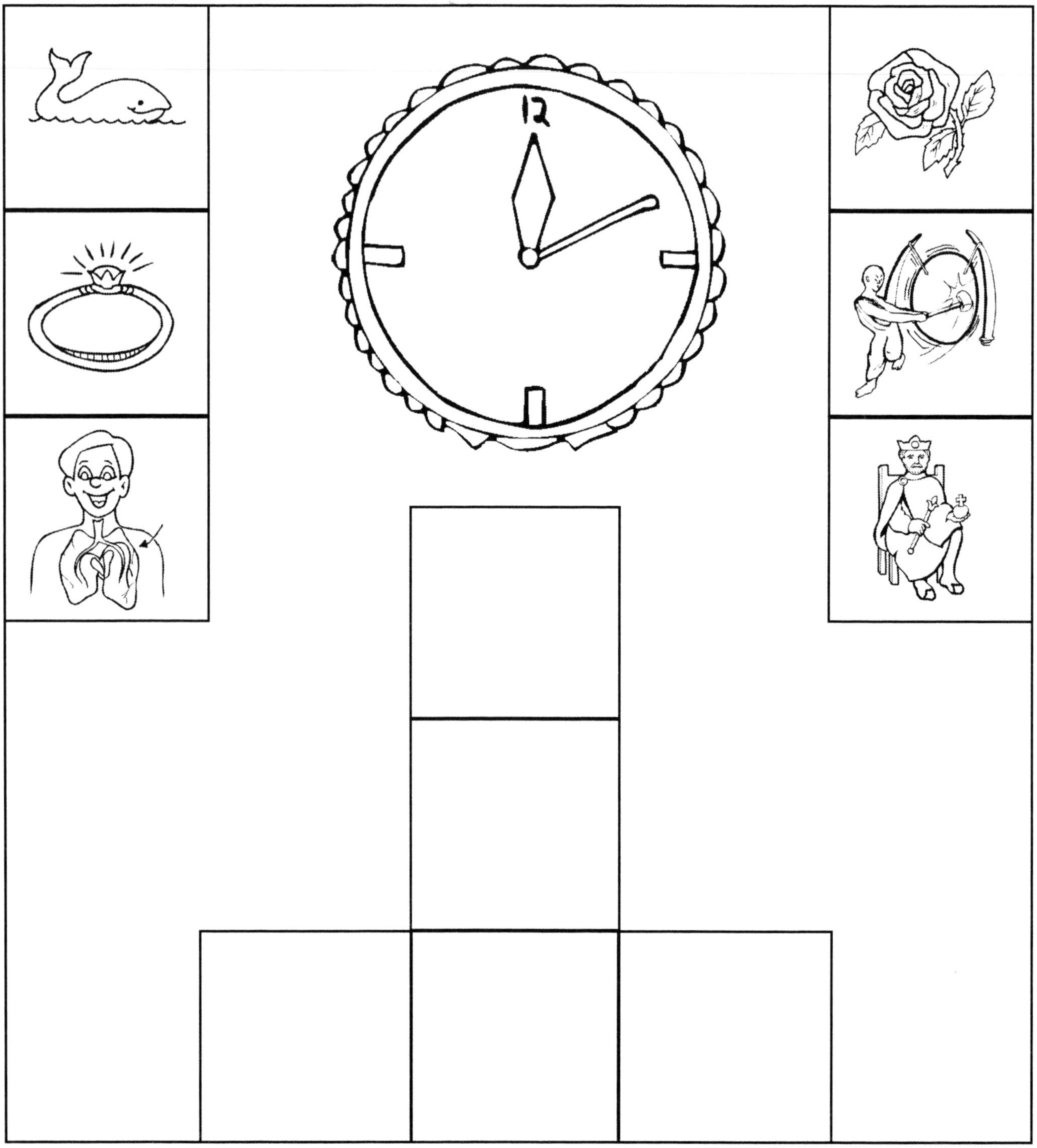

CHAPTER 7

Teaching the Sound of "igh"

Picture Popcorn

Materials:
- picture cards of things with the sound "igh"
- scissors
- timer (optional)

Preparation: This activity will require picture cards. You can make your own from the "word list" on page 61, or print out the PDFs found at: www.SongsThatTeach.com/phonics. Only cut out the pictures that have an "igh" in them (optional). Laminate them (optional).

How it Works: Give each student a picture card while the class sits in a circle. Give the students a moment to look at their picture and sound out their word. When everyone is ready, one student stands up, says their word and sits back down. The adjacent student does the same and so on until every student in the circle has had their turn. Then each student passes their picture card left, right or across and plays again. A timer can be used as an extra challenge.

Rhyming Picture Chain

Materials:
- picture cards
- glue

Preparation: This activity will require picture cards. You can make your own from the "word list" on page 61, or print out the PDFs found at: www.SongsThatTeach.com/phonics. Cut them out. Laminate them (optional). Divide the class up into groups.

How it Works: Give each group a set of picture cards with the "igh" sound and several other picture cards which do not have the "igh" sound. Have the students make a chain of only rhyming picture cards which have the "igh" sound. They can then color them and present them to you by saying what each picture is. Every word should rhyme.

CHAPTER 7

Night Light ("igh")

chorus 2x:

The letters "igh" make the long "i"
sound: / ī /, / ī /, / ī /
The letters "igh" make the long "i"
sound: / ī /, / ī /, / ī /

/ ī / is the sound in the middle of: right, night, light.
/ ī / is the sound at the end of: high.
/ ī /, / ī /, / ī /

The letters "igh" make the long "i"
sound: / ī /, / ī /, / ī /
The letters "igh" make the long "i"
sound: / ī /, / ī /, / ī /

/ ī / is the sound in the middle of: right, night, light.
/ ī / is the sound at the end of: high.
/ ī /, / ī /, / ī /

r-igh-t, right, br-igh-t, bright
n-igh-t, night, l-igh-t, light

I like a light
in the night, to be
bright, bright, bright.

A bright, light
feels right
in the dark night.

But, oh! I
sigh if the
light's too bright.

I need my
sleep and turn
off the light.

chorus:

The letters "igh" make the long "i"
sound: / ī /, / ī /, / ī /
The letters "igh" make the long "i"
sound: / ī /, / ī /, / ī /

/ ī / is the sound in the middle of: right, night, light.
/ ī / is the sound at the end of: high.
/ ī /, / ī /, / ī /

Name: _____

Mike and his Night Light

Mike uses a night light to help him sleep. Which of his dreams have a picture of an "igh" word in them? Indicate which pictures have an "igh" sound in their name by coloring them.

Name: _____

Which Light is Right?
Choose the right light by coloring the lightbulb that has a picture of an "igh" word in it.

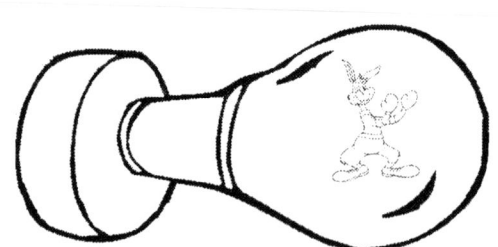
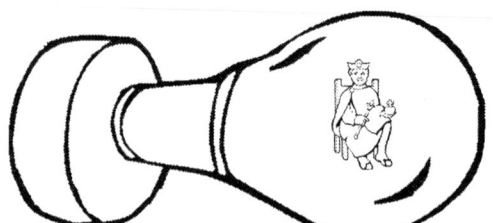
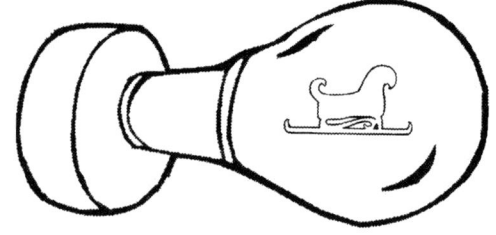
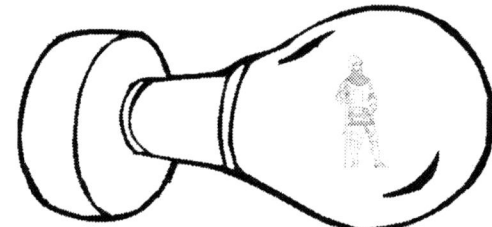
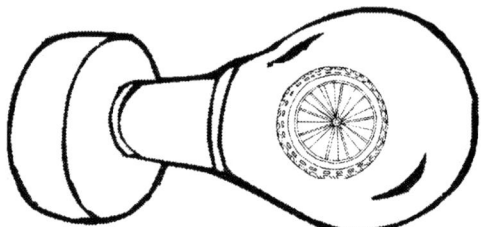
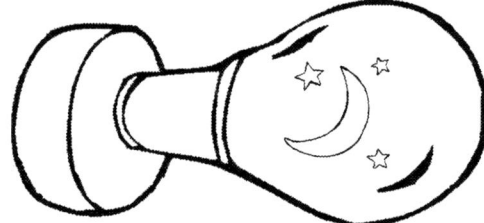

CHAPTER 8

Teaching the Sound of "oi"

Making Noise with "oi"

Materials: none

Preparation: none

How it Works: Choose a theme such as barnyard animals. Sing: "We'll be listening for some words that have "oi", "oi"
If you're ready for some noise say "oi", "oi".
If you really think you're ready and you want to make some noise, then listen for the words that have an "oi", "oi"".
Say "oi" words as well as non-"oi" words.
Have the students make some noise to the theme chosen whenever they hear the "oi" sound.

Building Words

Materials :
- chalk
- list of words with the "oi" sound

Preparation: None

How it Works: Begin by writing a letter on the chalkboard. Have the students sound it out. Add another letter and again have the students blend the sounds together while sounding it out. Continue doing this until the entire word in written on the board. Repeat this activity with many words having the particular target sound of "oi".

CHAPTER 8

Singing "oi" Words ("oi")

chorus 2x:

The letters "oi" make the sound:
/oi/, /oi/, /oi/.
The letters "oi" make the sound:
/oi/, /oi/, /oi/.

/oi/ is the first sound in: oil.
/oi/ is in the middle of: boil, broil.
The letters "oi" make the sound:
/oi/, /oi/, /oi/.

The letters "oi" make the sound:
/oi/, /oi/, /oi/.
The letters "oi" make the sound:
/oi/, /oi/, /oi/.

/oi/ is the first sound in: oil.
/oi/ is in the middle of: boil, broil.
The letters "oi" make the sound:
/oi/, /oi/, /oi/.

br-oi-l, broil, c-oi-l, coil
p-oi-n-t, point, f-oi-l, foil.

Join me in the kitchen.
I've pasta to boil.
In the water add a drop
of cooking oil.

Ice-cream in the freezer
so it will not spoil.
Cover up the cookies
with silver foil.

Would you like a cookie
that is nice and moist?
Chocolate or vanilla?
It's your choice.

Let's have a party.
Sing and make some noise;
all the happy voices
of girls and boys.

chorus 2x:

The letters "oi" make the sound:
/oi/, /oi/, /oi/.
The letters "oi" make the sound:
/oi/, /oi/, /oi/.

/oi/ is the first sound in: oil
/oi/ is in the middle of: boil, broil
The letters "oi" make the sound:
/oi/, /oi/, /oi/.

The letters "oi" make the sound:
/oi/, /oi/, /oi/.
The letters "oi" make the sound:
/oi/, /oi/, /oi/.

/oi/ is the first sound in: oil
/oi/ is in the middle of: boil, broil
The letters "oi" make the sound:
/oi/, /oi/, /oi/.

Name: _____

Finish the Sentence

Sound out the picture. Find the word that completes the sentence at the bottom of the page. Write it in the blank space. Read out the entire sentence.

Lucy has a nice singing _____ .

The _____ is used for planting.

Water will _____ when it is hot.

This _____ is in a bottle.

My piggybank has one _____ in it.

Word Bank				
boil	soil	oil	voice	coin

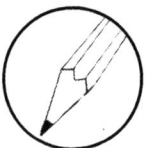

Name: _____

Birthday Party

Mark is having his birthday party but he and his friends need your help. They need to find out which of the pictures have an "oi" word in in it. Color the "oi" pictures to show them.

Teaching the Sounds of "ay" and "oy"

Building Towers

Materials:
- picture cards or word cards
- masking tape
- timer (optional)

Preparation: This activity will require picture cards. When choosing picture cards containing the target sounds "ay" or "oy", other pictures may also be chosen. You can make your own from the "word list" on page 61, or print out the PDFs found at: www.SongsThatTeach.com/phonics. Create word cards out of paper by simply cutting out rectangles and writing words with and without the target sound in them.

How it Works: Divide the class into two groups, the "ay" group and "oy" group. Spread the picture / word cards over a table. Have the students from each group find as many cards that contain their target sound and tape them to the board one on top of each other, creating a tower. The group with the largest tower after a certain amount of time wins. Cards in the tower that do not contain the target sound should be removed by you.

Proper Endings

Materials:
- chalk

Preparation: Create a list of "ay" and "oy" words

How it Works: Write a letter or series of letters on the chalkboard that will create a word with the "ay" or "oy" target sound in it. Without writing the actual target sound, leave a blank space and ask a volunteer to come up to the board and add the proper target sound and pronounce the word.

CHAPTER 9

Troy and Ray ("ay" and "oy")

chorus:

The letters "ay" make the sound / ā /
/ ā /, / ā /, / ā /.
The letters "ay" make the sound / ā /
/ ā /, / ā /, / ā /.

/ ā / can be found in: day, play.
/ ā / can be found in: stay, May.
The letters "ay" make the sound / ā /
/ ā /, / ā /, / ā /.

d-ay, day, pl-ay, play
st-ay, stay, R-ay, Ray

The letters "oy" make the sound: /oi/,
/oi/, /oi/, /oi/.
The letters "oy" make the sound: /oi/,
/oi/, /oi/, /oi/.
/oi/ can be found in: boy, joy.
/oi/ can be found in: toy, Roy.
The letters "oy" make the sound: /oi/
/oi/, /oi/, /oi/.

b-oy, boy, j-oy, joy
t-oy, toy, R-oy, Roy

One gray day
in the month of May,
a boy named Troy
went out to play.

Troy had a toy,
his very best toy;
a toy that gave Troy
lots of joy.

Troy met a boy.
His name was Ray.
Ray said, "Say, Troy
I like that toy."

The two boys played.
Troy and Ray,
with Troy's toy
on a gray May day.

chorus:

The letters "ay" make the sound / ā /
/ ā /, / ā /, / ā /.
The letters "ay" make the sound / ā /
/ ā /, / ā /, / ā /.

/ ā / can be found in: day, play.
/ ā / can be found in: stay, May.
The letters "ay" make the sound / ā /
/ ā /, / ā /, / ā /.

Name: _____

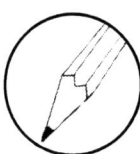

Missing Letters

Sound out each picture. Fill in the missing letters. Trace each word.
Color the pictures that have the "ay" or "oy" sound in them.

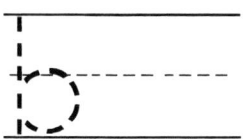 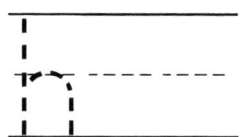 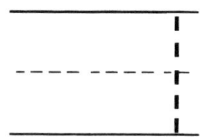

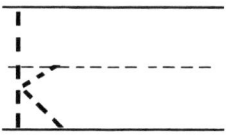 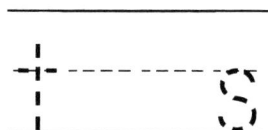 

Finish the Sentence

Sound out the picture. Find the word that completes the sentence at the bottom of the page. Write it in the blank space. Read out the entire sentence.

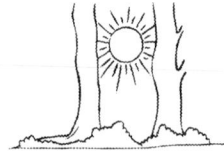 It was sunny outside the other _____.

An _____ lives in a shell in the ocean.

 There are many _____ in the toybox.

A horse eats _____.

 Lynn won the game.
She jumped up with _____.

Word Bank				
oyster	day	toys	joy	hay

CHAPTER 10

Teaching the Sounds of "ow" and "ou"

Hula-Hoop Phonics

Materials: • hula-hoops

Preparation: This activity will require picture cards. You can make your own from the "word list" on page 61, or print out the PDFs found at: www.SongsThatTeach.com/phonics. Place half as many hula-hoops as there are students on the floor. Assign a pair of students to each hula-hoop. Choose the target sounds "ow" and "ou". Assign a different one to each student.

How it Works: Read out words from the word list. Each pair of students stands just outside their hula-hoop. If a student hears their target sound, they jump into the hula-hoop unless they are already inside. If they do not hear their target sound, they jump out of the hula-hoop unless they are already outside.

Baskets

Materials:
• picture cards
• two baskets

Preparation: This activity will require picture cards. You can make your own from the "word list" on page 61, or print out the PDFs found at: www.SongsThatTeach.com/phonics. Cut out all the "ow" and "ou" picture cards as well as an equal amount of picture cards that do not contain the "ow" or "ou" spelling. Label one basket "ow" and the other "ou".

How it Works: Spread the picture cards across a table or the floor. Have the students pick up a picture card, read it out and place it in the correct basket.

CHAPTER 10

Round and Round ("ow" & "ou")

chorus:

The combinations "ow" and "ou" both make the sound /ou/, /ou/.
The combinations "ow" and "ou" both make the sound /ou/, /ou/.
The combinations "ow" and "ou" both make the sound /ou/, /ou/.
The combinations "ow" and "ou" both make the sound /ou/, /ou/.

chorus:

The combinations "ow" and "ou" both make the sound /ou/, /ou/.
The combinations "ow" and "ou" both make the sound /ou/, /ou/.
The combinations "ow" and "ou" both make the sound /ou/, /ou/.
The combinations "ow" and "ou" both make the sound /ou/, /ou/.

/ou/ is the first sound in: out, ouch.
/ou/ is the middle sound of: brown, frown, clown.
/ou/ is the end sound of: cow, how, now.
"ow" and "ou", /ou/, /ou/, /ou/.

ou-t, ou-t, out
br-ow-n, br-ow-n, brown
c-ow, c-ow, cow
s-ou-nd, s-ou-nd, sound.

Round and round
up and down
I ride my bike
all over town.

Feeling proud.
I shout out loud.
How fast I go
across the ground.

I do not pout
or scowl or frown.
My mouth just shouts
a happy sound.

Now I have
to turn around
and go back home
safe and sound.

Name: _____

Missing Letters

Sound out each picture. Fill in the missing letters. Trace each word.
Color the pictures that have the "ou" sound.

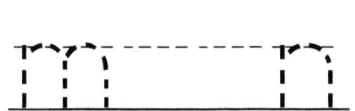 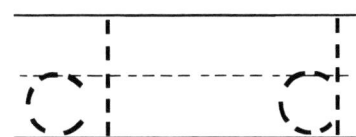 

m___n   cl__d   m__se

co___   h__se   sh__t

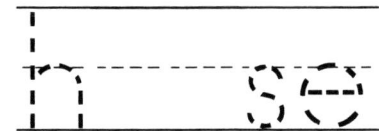 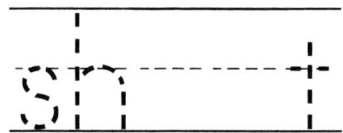

Name: _____

Finish the Sentence

Sound out the picture. Find the word that completes the sentence at the bottom of the page. Write it in the blank space. Read out the entire sentence.

 Lucy picked a nice green _____ .

Mark played over at Mike's _____ .

 The _____ ate the cheese.

"Hoot, hoot", said the _____ .

The _____ gave me a balloon.

Word Bank				
mouse	flower	house	clown	owl

CHAPTER 11

Teaching the Sounds of "k", Hard "c" and Soft "c"

Racing Cars

Materials:
- picture cards
- chalk
- scissors

Preparation: This activity will require picture cards. You can make your own from the "word list" on page 61, or print out the PDFs found at: www.SongsThatTeach.com/phonics. Cut them out and keep them together in a pile. Draw a series of vertical lines on the chalkboard. On the very left, draw two racecars which will be moving across the lines to the right.

How it Works: Divide the class into two equal groups — one for each racecar. Showing and pronouncing each picture card, have the students from one group decide whether the word on the picture card has a "soft c" a "hard c" or no "c". If successful, move their car over by one vertical line, otherwise, their car stays where it was. The first group to have their car cross the finish line wins.

Who Stole the Cookies from the Cookie Jar?

Materials:
- picture cards,
- two jars or plastic cups
- construction paper,
- scissors and glue
- marker

Preparation: This activity will require picture cards. You can make your own from the "word list" on page 61, or print out the PDFs found at: www.SongsThatTeach.com/phonics. Cut them out. Using the marker, label a jar/cup soft c and the other hard c. Cut out circles out of construction paper to be the cookies. Paste one picture card per cookie. Hide the cookies throughout the classroom.

How it Works: Have the students try to find as many cookies as they can. Once finished finding the cookies, have them approach you one by one, say the word illustrated by the picture card out loud and tell you which jar/cup it belongs to. They are then allowed to place it in the cookie jar.

CHAPTER 11

"k", Hard "c" and Soft "c"

Hard "c" and "k" both make the sound /k/.
Hard "c" and "k" both make the sound /k/.
crispy, crunchy, kiss, can
We make the /k/ sound when we can.
crispy, crunchy, kiss, can
We make the /k/ sound when we can.

Hard "c" and "k" both make the sound /k/.
Hard "c" and "k" both make the sound /k/.
crispy, crunchy, kiss, can
We make the /k/ sound when we can.
crispy, crunchy, kiss, can
We make the /k/ sound when we can.

c-a-t, c-a-t, c-a-t, cat
c-l-a-m, c-l-a-m, c-l-a-m, clam
k-i-d, k-i-d, k-i-d, kid
k-i-ck, k-i-ck, k-i-ck, kick

Soft "c" sounds like "s":
/s/, /s/, /s/.
Soft "c" sounds like "s":
/s/, /s/, /s/.
cent, city, ice, nice
Soft "c" sounds like "s".
cent, city, ice, nice
Soft "c" sounds like "s".

Soft "c" sounds like "s":
/s/, /s/, /s/.
Soft "c" sounds like "s":
/s/, /s/, /s/.
cent, city, ice, nice
Soft "c" sounds like "s".
cent, city, ice, nice
Soft "c" sounds like "s".

tw-i-ce, tw-i-ce, tw-i-ce, twice
f-e-n-ce, f-e-n-ce, f-e-n-ce, fence
m-i-ce, m-i-ce, m-i-ce, mice
pr-i-ce, pr-i-ce, pr-i-ce, price

My cat Clem cooks clams for lunch.
Clem eats his clams with a crunch.
Clem keeps his clams in a clean cup.
Counts his clams then eats them up.

Clem cooks clams with lots of spice,
He also slices them on ice.
He does not feed his clams to mice.
Clem does not think mice are nice.

Hard "c" and "k" both make the sound /k/.
Hard "c" and "k" both make the sound /k/.
crispy, crunchy, kiss, can
We make the /k/ sound when we can.
crispy, crunchy, kiss, can
We make the /k/ sound when we can.

Soft "c" sounds like "s":
/s/, /s/, /s/.
Soft "c" sounds like "s":
/s/, /s/, /s/.
cent, city, ice, nice
Soft "c" sounds like "s".
cent, city, ice, nice
Soft "c" sounds like "s".

Name: _____

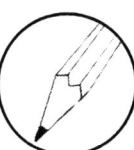

Clem the Cat

Clem is coloring his photo collection but he needs your help.

Color:
- the "hard c" words red,
- the "soft c" words yellow
- the "k" words green.

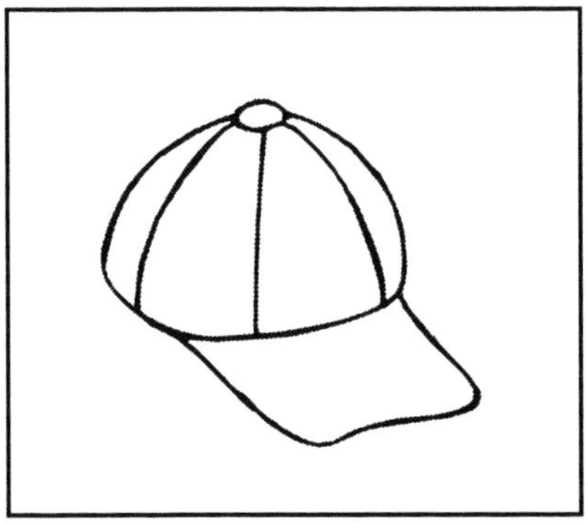

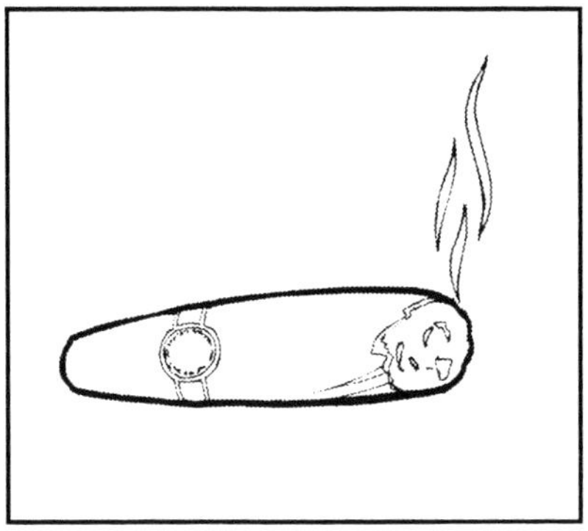

Crossword Puzzle

The pictures at the top represent words going across. The pictures at the bottom represent words going down. Sound out the pictures and fill in the blanks.

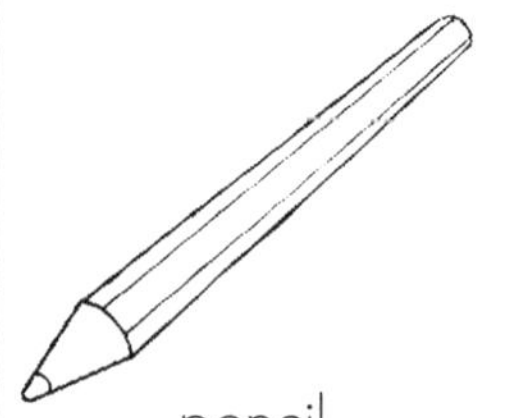

pencil 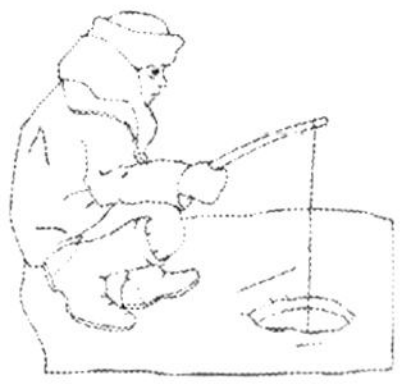   ice 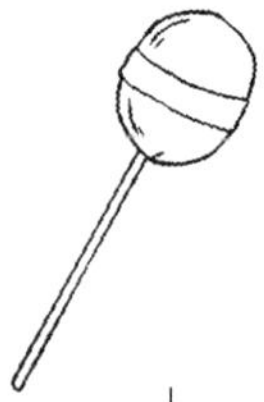   candy 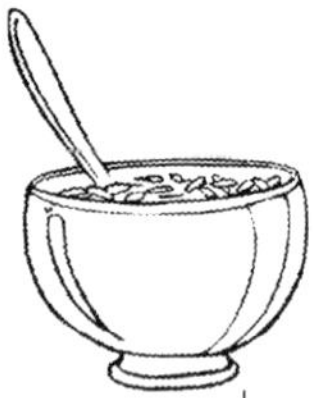   cereal 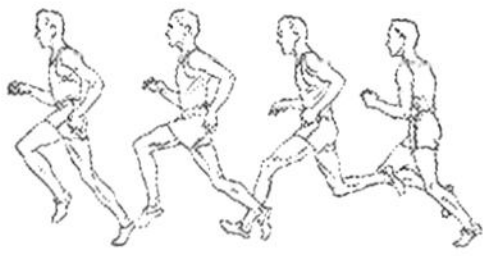   race

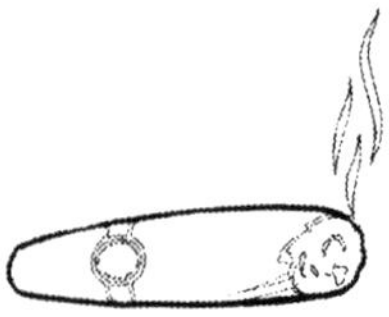

cigar

Across

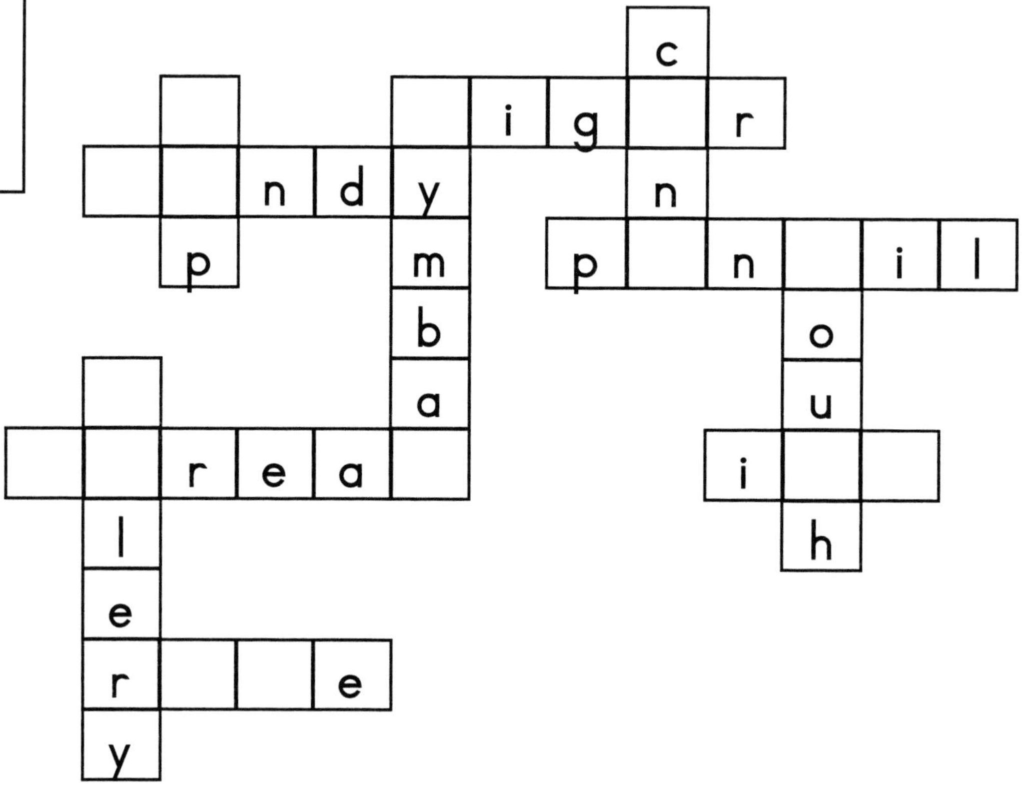

Down

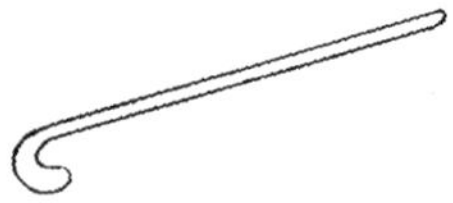

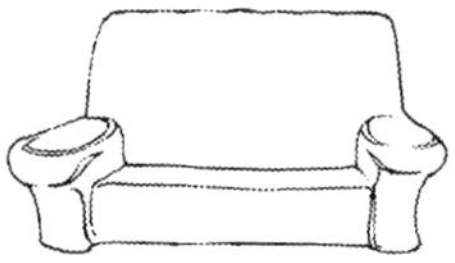

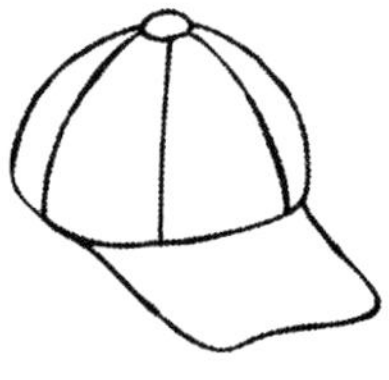

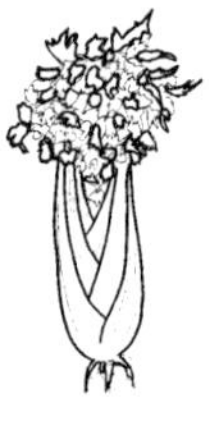

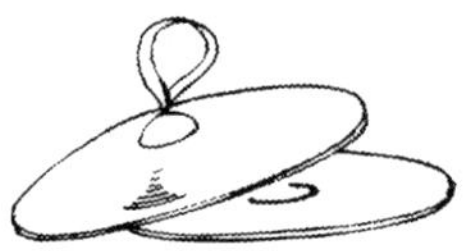

CHAPTER 12

Teaching the Sounds of Silent "h" and Silent "k"

Erase the Silent Letter

Materials:
- chalk
- chalk brush

Preparation: Write several words with the "silent h" and "silent k" as well as several other words the do not have "silent h" and "silent k" on the chalkboard.

How it Works: Have volunteers come up to the chalkboard and sound out a word. They are to then erase the first letter and sound out the word again. If the word sounds the same they say the word has a silent letter. If not, they write the letter back on the beginning of the word.

Knock Knock! Who's There?

Materials:
- accompanying audio CD

Preparation: This activity will require picture cards. You can make your own from the "word list" on page 61, or print out the PDFs found at: www.SongsThatTeach.com/phonics. Cue up the CD to the right track.

How it Works: Sing: "Knock Knock"
Students: "Who's There? Please give us a clue!"
Sing: "I am silent. I'm not heard. I'm the first letter of this word"
Say a word from the list.
Students: "You must be silent k (or h)!"
Repeat with other silent h/k words..

CHAPTER 12

Knock, Knock (Silent "h" and "k")

Knock! Knock! Who's there?
Please give me a clue!
I am silent. I'm not heard.
I'm the first letter of this word.
"knock", "knock"
You must be silent "k"!

Knock! Knock! Who's there?
Please give me a clue!
I am silent. I'm not heard.
I'm the first letter of this word.
"honest", "honest"
You must be silent "h"!

chorus:

*Letters can be tricky if
they're silent and not heard,
especially silent "h" and "k".
Let's try a few more words.*

Knock! Knock!
Who's there?
Please give me a clue!
I am silent. I'm not heard.
I'm the first letter of this word.
"knee", "knee"
You must be silent "k"!

Knock! Knock!
Who's there?
Please give me a clue!
I am silent. I'm not heard.
I'm the first letter of this word.
"hour", "hour"
You must be silent "h"!

chorus:

*Letters can be tricky if
they're silent and not heard,
especially silent "h" and "k".
Let's try a few more words.*

knock, knob, know, knee,
hour, heir, honesty.
knock, knob, know, knee,
hour, heir, honesty.

knock, knob, know, knee,
hour, heir, honesty.
knock, knob, know, knee,
hour, heir, honesty.

Name: _____

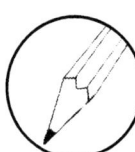

Missing Letters

Sound out each picture. Fill in the missing letter. Trace each word.
Color the pictures that have a "silent h" or "silent k" sound.

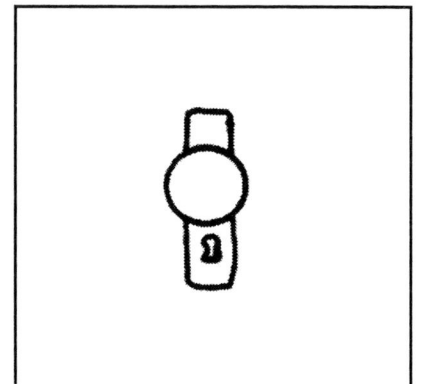

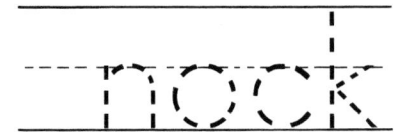

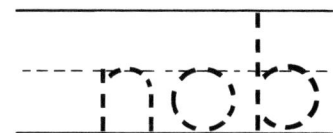

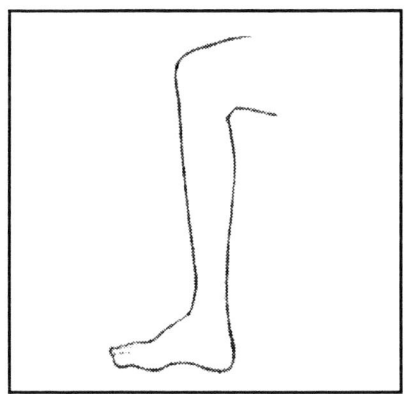

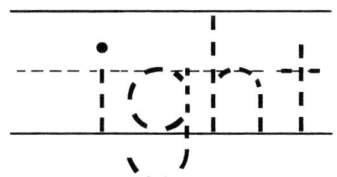
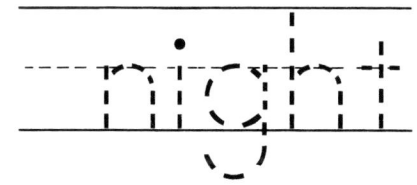

Sorting Balloons

Help the clown sort his balloons. Color the balloon:
– red, if it has a silent "h" word in it. or
– blue, if it has a silent "k" word in it.
– yellow, if it doesn't have either a silent "k" or "h"

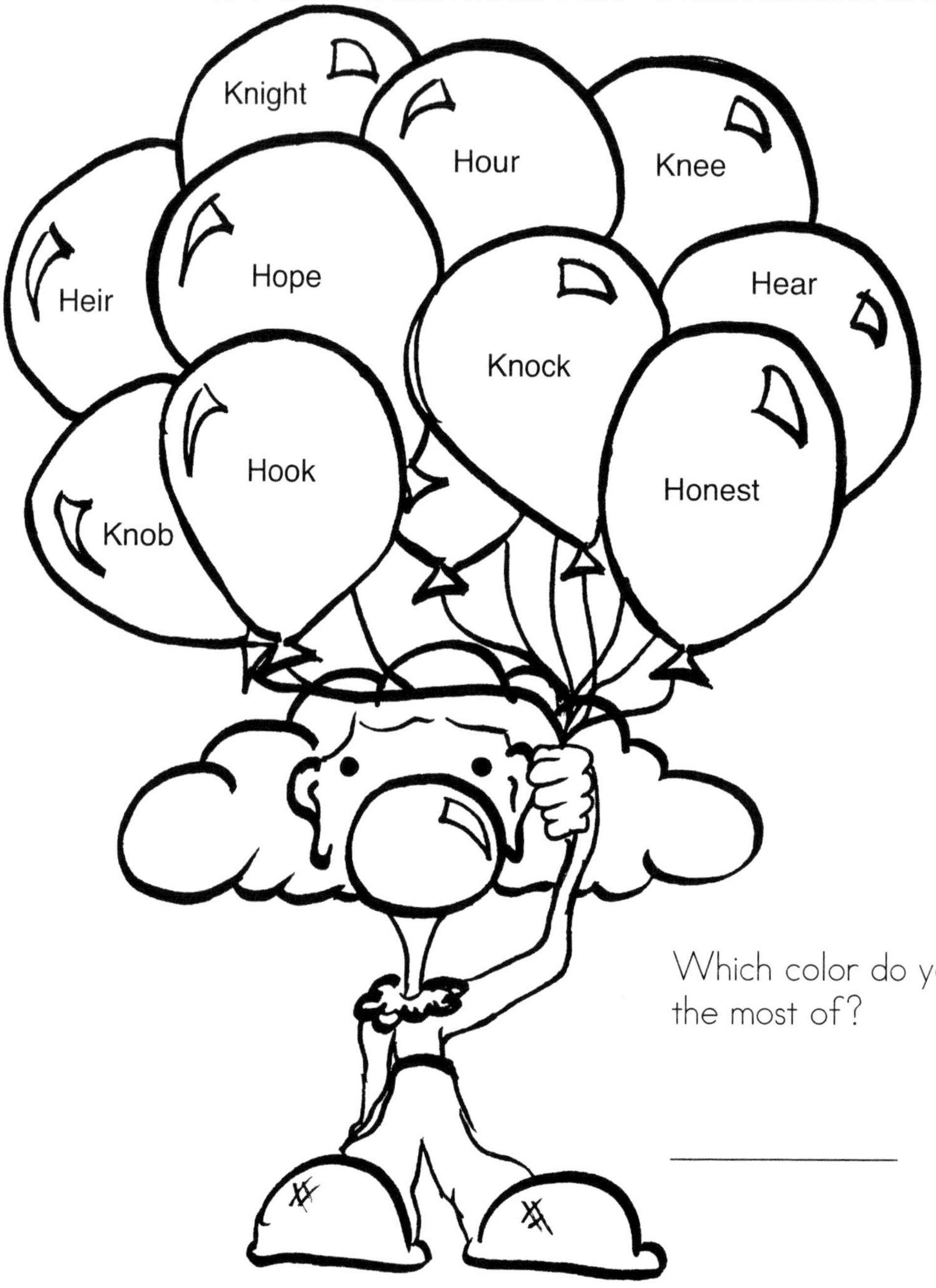

Knight
Hour
Knee
Heir
Hope
Hear
Knock
Hook
Honest
Knob

Which color do you see the most of?

_____

Name: _____

Knock, Knock

Who is there? Somebody is knocking on the doors. Can you answer right ones?
Color the doors that have a picture of a silent "k" or silent "h" word on it.

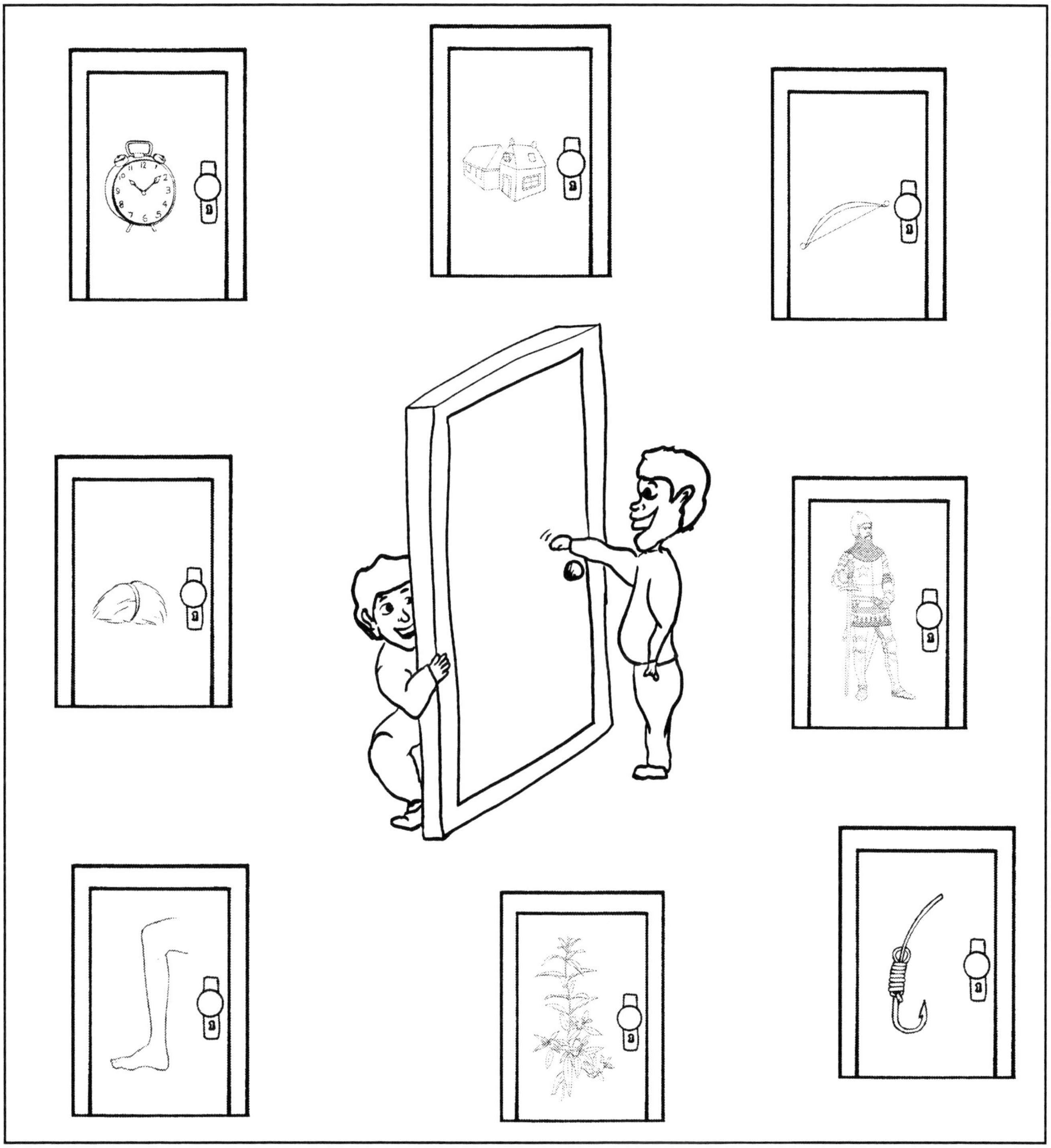

Name: _____

Missing Letters

Sound out each picture. Fill in the missing letter. Trace each word.

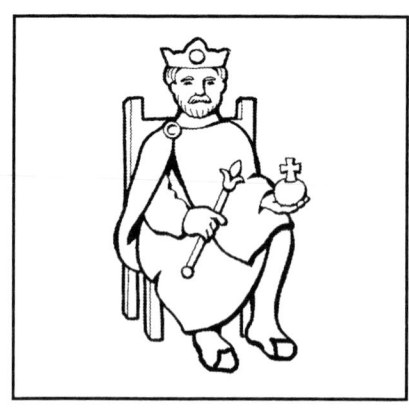

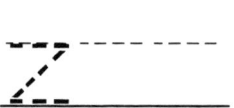
z _ _
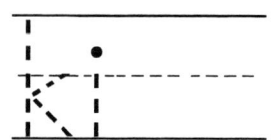
k i _

r _ s

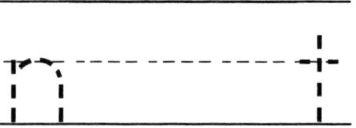
n _ t
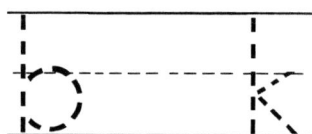
b _ k
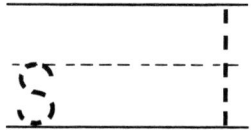
s _ t

Name: _____

Missing Letters

Sound out each picture. Fill in the missing letter. Trace each word.

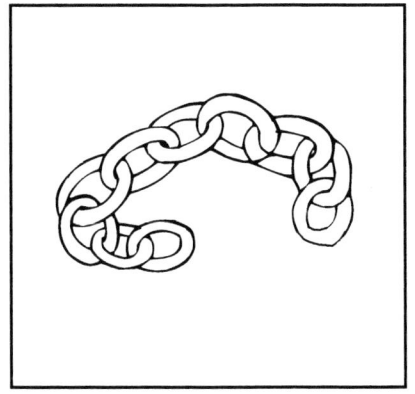  

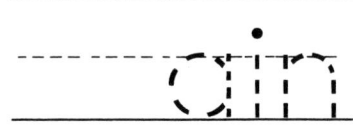 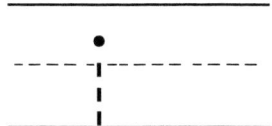 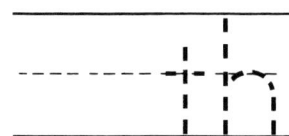

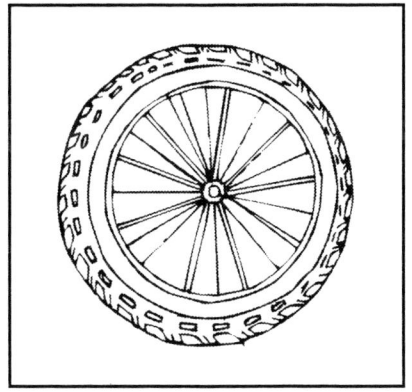 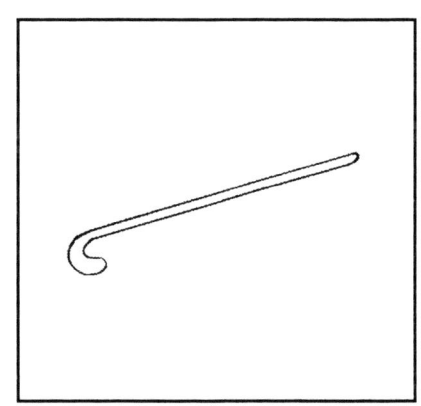 

 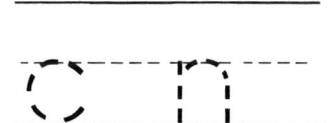

Sing and Learn Phonics, vol. 3   © 2014 Sara Jordan Publishing

Crossword Puzzle

The pictures above the crossword represent words going across. The pictures below the crossword represent words going down. Sound out the pictures. Fill in the blanks..

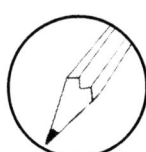

Missing Letters

Sound out each picture. Fill in the missing letters. Trace each word.

  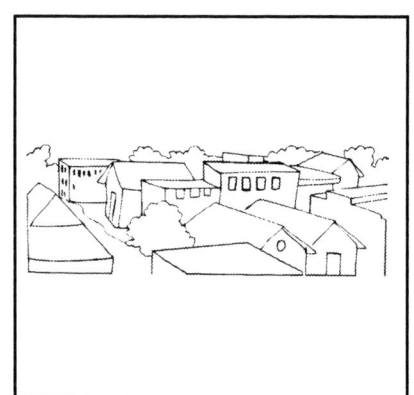

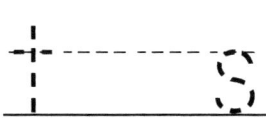 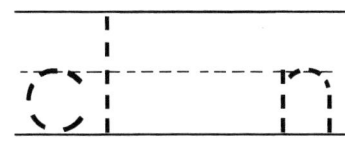 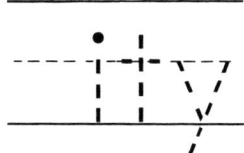

t_s   c_n   _ity

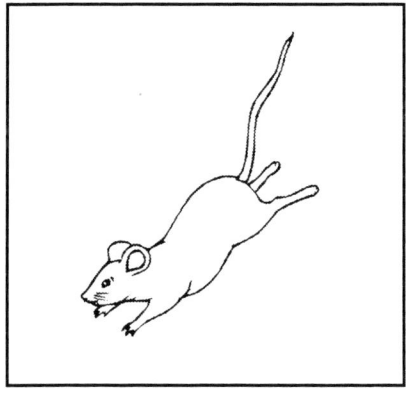 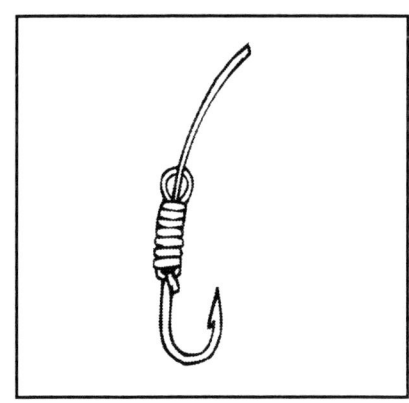 

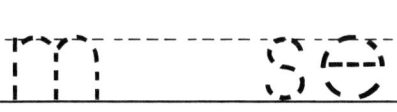 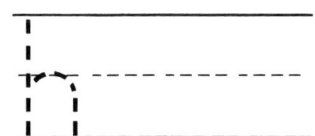

m_se   h_   _air

Name: _____

Juggling Jack

Sound out the pictures and color them. Cut and paste pictures that have an "ow" or "ou" sound around Jack so that he can juggle them.

COMPLETE LIST OF WORDS

Picture cards for the word list, supplementary phonics worksheets and activities can be found on our website at: www.sara-jordan.com/phonics

angel, ant, ape, apple, arm, ask, baby, bag, basket, bat, bat, bath, beach, bean, bed, bee, bell, belt, bench, bike, bird, blanket, blocks, boat, bone, book, boots, box, boy, branch, bread, brick, bridge, broom, bug, bunny, burger, bus, bush, cage, cake, can, candle, candy, cane, cap, car, carpet, castle, cat

cave, celery, cereal, chain, chair, cheese, chicken, chimney, church, cigar, city, claw, cloak, clock, closet, cloud, clover, clown, coat, coin, cone, cord, corn, couch, crab, cradle, crane, crayon, crib, cricket, crown, cry, cube, cup, cymbals, day, deer, ding-dong, dinosaur, dog, doll, dragon, dress, drink, drum, duck, egg, fan, farm, farmer

feather, feet, fence, fern, fire, fish, five, flag, flame, flashlight, flea, flower, flute, food, football, forest, fork, fox, frog, gate, gem, giant, giraffe, girl, globe, glue, goat, gong, grape, grass, gravy, grill, guitar, gum, ham, hammer, hand, hanger, happy, harp, hat, hay, hen, high, hook, horn, horse, house, ice, jacket

jail, jam, jar, jelly, jet, jug, juggle, juice, ketchup, key, kick, king, kite, knee, knight, knob, knock, ladder, lamp, leaf, leg, light, lion, lips, lock, log, look, lung, mail, map, marker, mask, mice, milk, mirror, mole, moon, mop, mouse, mule, neck, necklace, nest, net, night, nose, nurse, nuts, oil, owl

oyster, page, pail, pan, park, pay, peach, pen, pencil, pie, pig, pin, pizza, plane, plant, plate, pliers, plum, pocket, poison, pool, pot, price, prince, print, prize, propeller, quail, quake, queen, quick, quill, quit, quiz, race, rain, rake, rat, right, ring, rock, rocket, rose, rug, sailor, saw, scale, scarecrow, scarf, school

scooter, scream, seven, shark, sheep, shell, ship, shirt, shoes, shout, shower, sigh, sing, six, skate, skunk, sky, sled, sleep, sleigh, slide, small, smile, smoke, snail, snake, sneeze, snore, snow, soap, socks, soda, soil, space, spider, spoon, spy, squid, stage, stairs, star, stick, sun, swamp, swan, sweater, swim, swing, tape, teacher

teeth, ten, tent, thief, thin, think, thirty, thorn, three, ticket, toad, top, toys, tractor, train, trash, tree, troll, truck, trunk, tub, tube, turtle, umbrella, van, vet, vine, wagon, wall, watch, wave, web, whale, wheat, wheel, whip, whistle, wig, wings, winter, wood, x-ray, yak, yarn, yawn, yo-yo, zoo

About Sara Jordan Publishing

Sara Jordan Publishing is a recognized leader in the development of high quality, educational materials. Since 1990, the company has been producing educational resources designed to improve literacy, numeracy, language skills (English, French, Spanish and Mandarin), self-esteem, and interest in the world's diverse cultures. These award-winning programs are recommended by teachers and parents and enjoyed worldwide.

Sing and Learn Sight Words Series vol. 1-4
(Aligned with Common Core Curriculum)

This comprehensive program, introducing students to over 300 of the most commonly used sight words, has been created for students from K-3 but would be useful for beginning readers of any age.
The series is based on the list of 220 frequently used service words compiled by Edward William Dolch, Ph.D., and the related list of 95 high-frequency nouns. The words are presented in order of frequency. It is estimated that 50-75% of all words used in school books, library books, newspapers and magazines are included in the Dolch Basic Sight Vocabulary. The learning kits in this series include song CDs and feature ready-to-use classroom activities, lessons, reproducible worksheets and exercises based on the lessons taught in the songs. Recommended: K-Grade 3

Sing and Learn Phonics Series vol. 1-4
(Aligned with Common Core Curriculum)

Blending the best in educational research and practice, Sara Jordan's series, based on Synthetic Phonics, is a structured program providing students with the strategies needed to decode words through rhyming, blending and segmenting. Teachers and parents love the lessons, hands on activities and reproducible worksheets while children find the catchy, toe-tapping tunes fun. The resource books in this series feature ready-to-use classroom activities, lessons, reproducible worksheets and exercises based on the song CDs included in each book. Recommended: K-Grade 2

The Bilingual Songs and Activities Series

These resources will have your students speaking, singing and laughing in the new language. Each learning kit teaches different subjects ranging from the alphabet, counting, colors, opposites, shapes and sizes to gender, articles, adverbs, punctuation and question words. The activities and lyrics which can be photocopied by the classroom teacher include thematic, bilingual, lessons and exercises based on the lessons taught in the audio song CDs series. The activities and lessons are enhanced with cultural references to foreign geography, customs, traditional games, food, and holidays. Available in English-Spanish and English-French formats.

Bilingual Songs: English-Mandarin Chinese, vol. 1

Exciting songs in both English and Mandarin teach the alphabet (English and Pinyin), counting to 10, days of the week, months of the year, weather, seasons, colors, food, Chinese zodiac signs, parts of the body, clothing and family members. Includes reproducible lyrics book in English, Mandarin and Pinyin to aid pronunciation. The singers in English and Mandarin are native speakers. Music accompaniment tracks make singing along karaoke-style fun and class performances a snap.

The Math Unplugged Series
(Aligned with Common Core Curriculum)

This musical approach to math was created by teachers and is a great alternative to heavier rock and rap programs. It uses an interactive approach. Each learning kit includes a song CD with songs teaching the facts plus self-quizzing songs. The group activities and reproducible exercises are aligned with the Common Core Curriculum. The multiplication and division kits are especially designed to feature and review skip counting in the chorus of every song.

Thematic Songs for Learning Language
Great as an ESL resource! These songs and activities teach common expressions, modes of transportation, clothing, mealtime, weather, parts of the body, pets and rooms of the house. There is even a song teaching the correct use of prepositions!

Character Building Songs
Classroom teachers and music teachers alike will be delighted with this set of songs teaching generosity, responsibility, respect, honesty, etiquette, tolerance, empathy, courage, perseverance and optimism. Separate arrangements allow each song to be sung in unison, as a round or as a classroom performance. The reproducible lyrics book includes lessons and activities.

Lullabies Around the World
Winner of both a Parents' Choice Silver Award and a Directors' Choice Award. Featuring a dozen singers, each singing in his or her own native tongue. Includes Russian, Polish, Japanese, Mandarin, French, Spanish, Italian, Yiddish, African and American lullabies with their English translations. The accompanying lyrics book (which classroom teachers may reproduce) includes multicultural activities.

Celebrate the Human Race
Award-winning songs based on the lives and cultures of children whose homelands boast the Seven Natural Wonders of the World. This is an incredible resource. Each song is musically representative of the culture. Paper dolls and costumes are included in the reproducible lyrics book.

We would like to invite you to join the online community of teachers, parents, friends and associates who receive our electronic newsletter. Every two weeks we faithfully write up teaching ideas, related links and lesson plans based on one, two or even three of our songs. These are all sent, free of charge, along with the free song downloads to recipients of our newsletter.

To subscribe to our English newsletter, visit: www.SongsThatTeach.com.

To subscribe to our Spanish newsletter, visit: www.AprendeCantando.com